Cornerstones

Anthology 2b

Carolyn Farr   Jane Hutchison

Carol McGrail   Carol Pawlowski

gagelearning

Bias Consultant: Margaret Hoogeveen

Cover Illustration: Rob Johannsen

National Library of Canada Cataloguing in Publication Data

Main entry under title:

Gage cornerstones : Canadian language arts. Anthology, 2b

ISBN 0-7715-1243-0

1. Readers (Primary). I. Farr, Carolyn
II. Title: Cornerstones: Canadian language arts.
III. Title: Anthology, 2b.

PE1119.G234 2000   428.6   C99-932462-4

Acknowledgments

Every reasonable effort has been made to trace ownership of copyrighted material. Information that would enable the publisher to correct any reference or credit in future editions would be appreciated.

We acknowledge the financial support of the Government of Canada through the Book Publishing Industry Development Program for our publishing activities.

8 From My *Kokum Called Today* by Iris Loewen and Gloria Miller. Text © 1993 Iris Loewen. Illustrations © 1993 Gloria Miller. By permission of Pemmican Publications Inc. **18** "Stoops" by Mimi Brodsky Chenfeld, reprinted by permission of the author. **22** From *Each One Special* by Frieda Wishinsky and H. Werner Zimmermann. Text © 1998 Frieda Wishinsky. Illustrations © 1998 H. Werner Zimmermann. By permission of Orca Book Publishers. **38** Adapted from "Chimpanzees" *Chickadee* © 1999 with permission of the publisher, Bayard Presse Canada Inc., Toronto, Canada. **43** "Balloon" by Colleen Thibaudeau. © Colleen Thibaudeau. Reprinted by permission of the author. **48** From *A Balloon for Grandad* by Jane Ray and Nigel Gray first published in the UK by Orchard Books in 1994, a division of The Watts Publishing Group Limited, 96 Leonard Street, London EC2A 4XD. **62** Material from *Simple Machines* used by permission of Kids Can Press, Ltd., Toronto. Text © 1996 Deborah Hodge 1996. Photographs © Ray Boudreau 1996. **64** "Rachel's Boat" from *Looking for Holes: Poems*. Text © 1995 by Niko Scharer. Illustrations copyright © 1995 by Gary Clement. First published in Canada by Groundwood Books/ Douglas & MacIntyre. By permission of the publisher. **66** From *Follow the Water from Brook to Ocean* © 1991, Arthur Dorros. By permission of HarperCollins Children's Books, a division of HarperCollins Publishers. **76** Reprinted with permission from *Vroom! Vroom!* by Judy Press and Michael Kline. Text © 1997 Judy Press. Illustrations © 1997 Michael Kline. By permission of Williamson Publishing Company, Charlotte, VT 05445. **82** *Crazy for Canada* by Noa Schwartz, Mick Beaumont, and Susan Tebutt. Text © 1997, Noa Schwartz. Illustrations © 1997, Mick Beaumont and Susan Tebutt. By permission of Tumbleweed Press. **94** Material from *Canada's Maple Leaf: The Story of Our Flag* used by permission of Kids Can Press Ltd., Toronto. Text copyright © Anne-Maureen Owens and Jane Yealland 1999. Illustrations © Bill Slavin and Esperança Melo 1999. **96** From *To Be a Kid* Text © 1999 SHAKTI for Children. Used by permission of Charlesbridge Publishing. All rights reserved. **102** From *This Is the Way We Go to School* by Edith Baer, illustrated by Steve Björkman. Text © 1990 by Edith Baer, illustrations © 1990 by Steven Björkman. Reprinted by permission of Scholastic Inc. **108** From *Mabel Murple* by Sheree Fitch (poetry) and Maryann Kovalski (illustrations) © 1995 Sheree Fitch and Darcia Labrosse. Reprinted with permission of Doubleday Canada Limited. **117** "On a Day in Summer" by Aileen Fisher © 1981 Aileen Fisher. Used by permission of Marian Reiner for the author.

120 From *Painted Words* by Aliki Brandenberg. © 1988 by Aliki Brandenberg. Published by Greenwillow. Reprinted by permission of HarperCollins Children's Books, a division of HarperCollins Publishers. **134** Adapted from "Brand New Buddies" *Chickadee* © 1999 with permission of the publisher, Bayard Presse Canada Inc., Toronto, Canada. **136** From *Dear Mr. Blueberry* by Simon James. © 1991 by Simon James. By permission of Candlewick Press. **142** "Come Quick" from *Small Plays for Special Days*. Text © 1977 by Sue Alexander. Reprinted by permission of Clarion Books/Houghton Mifflin Company. All rights reserved. **146–147** "Bedbunnies" from *Rebus Riot*. Text © 1997 by Bonnie Christensen. By permission of Dial Books for Young Readers, a division of Penguin Putnam Inc. **148** "Firefly Song" from *Myth of Hiawatha* by Henry Schoolcraft, translated by Henry Schoolcraft, published by J. B. Lippincott, Philadelphia: 1856. **150** From *Reading Grows* by Ellen B. Senisi. © 1999 Ellen B. Senisi. By permission of Albert Whitman & Company. **159** "The Inchworm" from *Insectlopedia* by Douglas Florian © 1998 Douglas Florian. By permission of Harcourt Inc.

Photo Credits
38 upper left Renée Lynn/Tony Stone Images, **right** Tim Davis/Tony Stone Images; **39 background** Renée Lynn/Tony Stone Images; **44 background** Brian Atkinson, **top right** W.E.R. Photo, **lower left** Bob Rowan; Progressive Image/CORBIS; **45 background** Brian Atkinson/New Brunswick Department of Tourism, **left** Brian Atkinson/New Brunswick Department of Tourism, **lower right** Richard Cummins/CORBIS ; **46 background** Brian Atkinson/New Brunswick Department of Tourism, **top** Chad Ehlers/International Stock; **47 top** Kay Milton, **bottom** Artbase; **74 top and bottom** Artbase; **75 top, middle** and **bottom** Artbase; **92 middle, 93 top** courtesy of the Royal Canadian Mint; **92 bottom** Dave Starrett; **96** From *To Be a Kid* 1999 SHAKTI for Children. Photographs © (by page counterclockwise from upper left): **96** Steven G. Herbert, John D. Ivanko; **97** Mary Altier, Stephen Chicoine, Elaine Little; **98** John D. Ivanko, Mary Altier; **99** Christopher Szell, Watson/Childreach, John D. Ivanko; **100** Stephen Chicoine, John Warren; **101** Stephen Chicoine, International Public Affairs Branch of the DFAT, Elaine Little. Used by permission of Charlesbridge Publishing. All rights reserved. **118-119** Dave Starrett; **134** Daniel Pangbourne/Masterfile; **135** Ian Crysler; **150-157** Ellen B. Sensi.

Illustrations
6-7 Farida Zaman; **18-21** Joe Weissmann; **40, 79 top** John Etheridge; **41, 115, 142-145, 158 top** Scot Ritchie; **42-43** Tomio Nitto; **64-64** Jackie Besteman; **76-77** Anne Stanley; **78 top** Bill Suddick, **bottom** Dayle Dodwell; **80-81** Sue Todd; **116-117** Marion Stuck; **118-119** Kim Lafave; **146-147, 159** Chum McLeod; **148-149** Margot Thompson; **158 bottom** Dayle Dodwell.

Cornerstones Development Team

WRITING TEAM
Carolyn Farr
Jane Hutchison
Carol McGrail
Carol Pawlowski

EDITORIAL TEAM
GAGE EDITORIAL
Joe Banel
Elizabeth Long
Darleen Rotozinski

FIRST FOLIO RESOURCE GROUP, INC.
Fran Cohen
Maggie MacDonald
Jane McWhinney
Alison Reid
Tara Steele

GAGE PRODUCTION
Anna Kress
Bev Crann

DESIGN, ART DIRECTION & ELECTRONIC ASSEMBLY
Pronk&Associates/David Montle

ADVISORY TEAM
Jane Abernethy, Chipman & Fredericton SD, NB
Gwen Bartnik, Vancouver SB, BC
Susan Boehnke, Durham DSB, ON
Lisa Bond, Catholic Independent Schools of Vancouver Archdiocese, BC
Marg Craig, Lambton Kent DSB, ON
Laurel Galt, Durham DSB, ON
Gloria Gustafson, Coquitlam DSB, BC
Lise Hawkins, Toronto DSB, ON
Carol Hryniuk-Adamov, Winnipeg SD, MB
Sharon Kinakin, Langley SD #35, BC
Jane Koberstein, Mission DSB, BC
Irene Kovats, Calgary CSSB, AB
Martin MacDonald, Strait Regional SB, NS
Sharon Morris, Toronto CDSB, ON
Cheryl Norman, Delta SD #37, BC
Jennifer Pinches, Calgary CSD, AB
Joanne Pizzuto, Windsor DSB, ON
Pearl Reimer, Edmonton PSB, AB
Lydia Renahan, Peel DSB, ON
Maureen Rodniski, Winnipeg SD, MB
Patricia Rooney, Wellington County CDSB, ON
Barbara Rushton, Annapolis Valley Regional SB, NS
Lynn Strangway, Simcoe DSB, ON
Anna Totten, Toronto CDSB, ON
Doreen M. Valverde, Southwest Regional SB, NS
Suzanne Witkin, Toronto DSB, ON

Contents

PERSONAL FOCUS
My Family and Friends

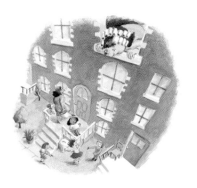

Where Families Live by Carol McGrail, Carolyn Farr **7**

My Kokum Called Today by Iris Loewen. Pictures by Gloria Miller **8**

Stoops by Mimi Brodsky Chenfeld **18**

Each One Special by Frieda Wishinsky. Pictures by H. Werner Zimmermann **22**

Friendly Chimps from *Chickadee* **38**

Responding to My Family and Friends Created by Carolyn Farr **40**

SCIENCE FOCUS
Wind and Water

Balloon by Colleen Thibaudeau **43**

Balloon Fiesta by Tara Steele **44**

A Balloon for Grandad by Nigel Gray. Pictures by Jane Ray **48**

Twirling Toy by Deborah Hodge **62**

Rachel's Boat by Niko Scharer **64**

Follow the Water from Brook to Ocean by Arthur Dorros **66**

Wonderful Water by Evelyn Steinberg **74**

Sailboat by Judy Press. Pictures by Michael Kline **76**

Responding to Wind and Water Created by Carol McGrail **78**

SOCIAL STUDIES FOCUS

My Country, My World

✤ O Canada!   **81**

✤ Crazy for Canada by Noa Schwartz.
Pictures by Mick Beaumont and Susan Tebbutt   **82**

✤ Claudia's Coin by Tara Steele   **92**

✤ Canada's Maple Leaf by Ann-Maureen Owens
and Jane Yealland. Pictures by Bill Slavin and
Esperança Melo   **94**

To Be a Kid by Maya Ajmera and John D. Ivanko   **96**

This Is the Way We Go to School
by Edith Baer. Pictures by Steve Björkman   **102**

✤ Mabel Murple by Sheree Fitch.
Pictures by Maryann Kovalski   **108**

Responding to My Country, My World
Created by Carol Pawlowski   **114**

GENRE STUDY

Celebrate Reading

On a Day in Summer by Aileen Fisher   **117**

✤ Reading All Around Us by Jane Hutchison   **118**

Painted Words by Aliki Brandenberg   **120**

✤ Pen Pals from *Chickadee*   **134**

Dear Mr. Blueberry by Simon James   **136**

"Come Quick!" by Sue Alexander   **142**

Bedbunnies by Bonnie Christensen   **146**

Firefly Song an Ojibwa poem   **148**

Reading Grows by Ellen B. Senisi   **150**

Responding to Celebrate Reading
Created by Jane Hutchison   **158**

✤ Canadian Content

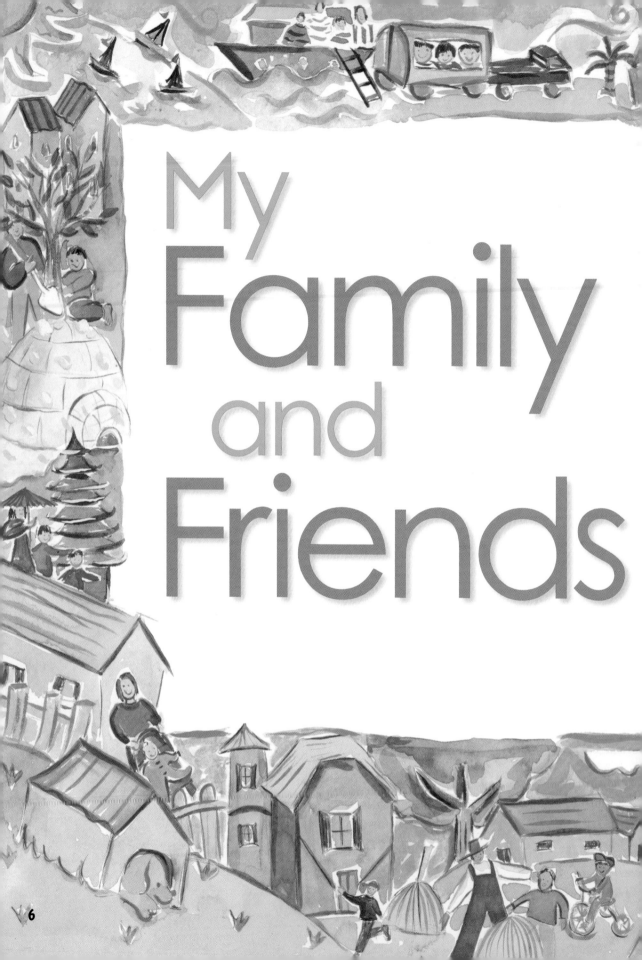

My Family and Friends

Where Families Live

Towering apartments scraping the sky,
Adobe huts in deserts dry,
Floating houseboats rocked by the seas,
And wooden houses shaded with trees,

Made of stone, of steel or bricks,
Of clay, of stucco, of mud or sticks,
In mountains, in jungles; on snow and on sand,
Are homes for families from every land.

7

My Kokum Called Today

by Iris Loewen
pictures by Gloria Miller

When I came home from school today, my Mom said, "Your Kokum called today. There's a round dance on the Reserve. She wants us to come home this weekend."

"Neeto!" I said, "Are we leaving right away?"

"Yes. So move it kid. We have a long way to go.
Hurry. Don't forget your new moccasins. You can
wear them to the dance."

My Mom and I live in a big city.

My Kokum lives on an
Indian Reserve 200 kilometres
away. My Kokum is Cree. "Kokum"
means Grandmother in Cree.

I bet you'd like my Kokum. She is the kindest
person I know. She always gives me a hug and a big
kiss when she sees me. I love her very much.

And round dances
are the greatest.

Everyone goes.

Really old people,
young people,
teeny tiny babies
and their families
go.

Everyone goes to a
round dance.

People come from many different Reserves.
We dance in a circle holding hands. The drummers
sing and drum all night. We dance until the sun
comes up.

"I can't wait to see my uncles and aunts and cousins. And we can see Aunt Alice's new baby. Hurry Mom, let's go! I'm so glad Kokum called today!"

Stoops

by **Mimi Brodsky Chenfeld**

My name is Anna and this is my seat on the third
step of our stoop. Next stoop, Sammy and Pedro
play stoop ball. The other kids jump double Dutch
and play hopscotch and bouncy balls on the street.
I am waiting for Kim.

"Hurry, Kim! I've got something to tell you,"
I holler up.

"What?" she hollers down from her fourth-floor window.

"I'll tell you when you come down," I yell. "Bring your jacks—I forgot mine."

Pedro and Sam throw the ball; it misses the step. It bounces into Mrs. Shapiro's lap, and she says, "Careful, boys."

She tosses it back and goes on talking to Mr. Gomez.

I scoot over to let Mrs. Brown by, as she bumps her grocery bags past me.

"Come on, Kim," I call again up to her window. The jump-rope kids jump.

"Come on, Kim," they yell.

Kim's aunt puts her head out the window.

"Not till she cleans the table," she calls.

"Clean it, Kim," I yell.

"Clean it, Kim," Pedro and Sammy tease.

"Clean it," the hopscotch kids call, hopping from square to square.

"Clean it." The jump-rope kids jump with each swing of the rope.

"Clean it," the bouncing-ball kids chant with each bounce of the ball.

"Tell your secret, Anna." The kids begin to clap, and now it is a song, a song about jump rope and jacks, hopscotch and bouncing balls, and the secrets of friends playing on the stoop of home.

Each One Special

by Frieda Wishinsky
pictures by H. Werner Zimmermann

PART 1

Harry was a cake decorator.

With a squeeze and a twist, he shaped roses, daisies, and forget-me-nots out of butter-cream icing.

With a squeeze and a twist, he spun marzipan toes on twirling ballerinas, cherry smiles on coconut clowns, and caramel trains chugging down chocolate tracks.

Every day after school Ben visited Harry at the bakery.

Sometimes Harry let Ben help decorate. Sometimes Ben swirled a petal on a flower or a smile on a face.

Ben loved helping Harry. He loved watching Harry make each cake different and each cake special.

Harry's customers loved his cakes too.

"Ooh," they applauded when Harry opened the cake box.

"Ahh," they sighed as Harry turned their cake from side to side.

"A masterpiece!" they proclaimed as they carefully carried their cake home.

Each year on Ben's birthday, Harry made Ben a special cake.

One year he made a raspberry rocketship landing on a walnut moon.

Another year he made a mint racing car striped in yellow and red.

But Ben's favourite cake was the tall mocha cowboy spinning a butterscotch lasso.

"Harry," said Ben, "you can make anything!" And Harry could.

Then one day the owner of Harry's bakery sold his shop. The new owners wanted new bakers.

"But I have thirty-five years of experience," Harry told them. "And each cake I make is different. Each cake is special."

"We want fast, not different," they told him.

"We want lots, not special," they said.

"We want young bakers, not old," they insisted.

Harry looked for a new job. But he couldn't find one.

Harry didn't know what to do.

"Go fishing," said Harry's wife Fran. But all Harry caught was a cold.

"Try golf," said Fran. But Harry hit everything except the golf ball.

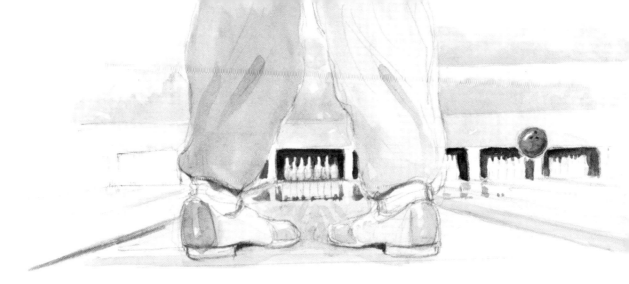

"How about bowling?" said Fran. But Harry's bowling balls bounced into the wrong lane.

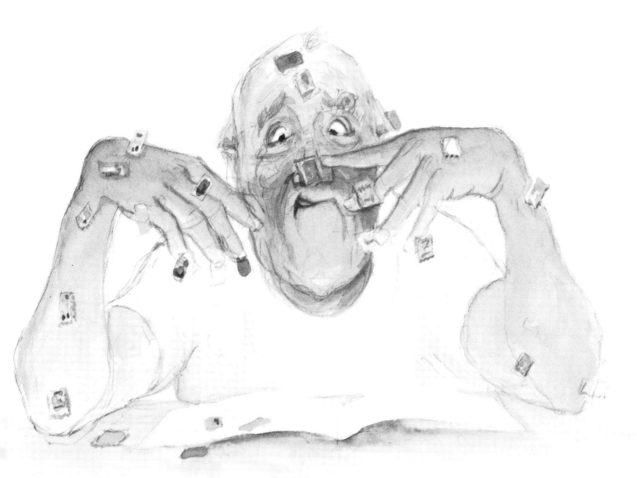

"Collect stamps," said Fran. But Harry liked to make things, not collect them.

PART 2

Soon all Harry did was sit in his blue chair and watch TV.

"He's not the same man," said Fran, her eyes full of tears.

"Harry is still Harry," Ben told her. "He just hasn't found what he wants to do."

But as Ben watched Harry sit in his chair, even Ben began to worry. He missed Harry's laughs as Harry shaped and squeezed. He missed Harry's smiles as customers *oohed* and *ahhed*. But most of all, he missed the old Harry.

Then one day Ben's mom bought him some clay.

Ben played with the clay. He made a bird and a cat. Then he tried to make a cowboy, but he couldn't.

So Ben took the clay over to Harry.

"Can you make a cowboy out of this clay?" he asked.

"What do I know about working with clay?" said Harry. "All I know is cakes."

"But Harry," said Ben, hugging him tight, "you can make anything!"

Harry smiled.

"All right," Harry said.
"Let's have a look at your clay."
   Harry picked up
a handful.

He squeezed it between his fingers.
He twisted it in his hands. He turned
it this way and that.

Slowly, slowly, a shape appeared.
"Harry!" Ben shouted. "It's a rose!"
"You're right!" said Harry. "It is!"

Harry took some more clay. He squeezed and twisted. He turned it this way and that.

"A daisy!" Ben shouted.

"Now watch this," said Harry.

In no time, a bouquet burst out of the clay.

"You're a magician, Harry," said Ben. "Now please make a cowboy!"

"A cowboy is not so easy," laughed Harry.

"But you can do it," Ben said. "I know you can."

"Then let's give it a try," said Harry, and he began to shape the clay. Soon a tall cowboy popped out of the clay, spinning a lasso.

"He's great!" said Ben. "But he needs a hat."

"Then give him one," said Harry, and he handed Ben a lump of clay.

Ben twisted and pulled the clay. He turned it this way and that till he shaped a tall hat. Carefully Ben placed it on the cowboy's head.

"I love it!" exclaimed Harry. "And I love this clay. It's fun. It's like butter-cream icing. It's like marzipan and caramel. I'm going to buy some clay."

The next day Harry bought two bags of clay.
Soon Harry was busy twisting and shaping. Beside
him, Ben twisted and shaped too.

It was not long before people
came to see Harry and Ben's
sculptures and to buy them.
And when they arrived, Ben
showed them around.

"Ooh! Ahh!" they exclaimed.
"What masterpieces!"

For just like Harry's cakes...
each sculpture was different.

Each one was special.

Friendly Chimps

A chimpanzee shows its friends how much it loves them by kissing, touching, and playing with them. It will also show its feelings by cleaning out ticks or dirt from its friend's hair. If you see a very clean chimp, you know it must have a lot of pals! Chimp friends might even take out splinters from each other's hands! *Yeouch!* Could you do that for your friend?

It's Hip to Skip

Jump and count, the skipper's ashore!
Add one more and keep the score.
When your number reaches four,
Everybody's out the door.

Create your own skipping activity with a
partner. Add a skipping chant. Try your
chant in the gym. Try your chant at recess.

Home Link Ask who in
your family
remembers an old
skipping rhyme. Have
your family member
teach you the chant.
Bring it to school and
share it with the class.

Grandpa Dough's recipe for modelling fun!

- 4 cups of flour
- 1 1/2 cups of water (add food colouring for colour)
- 1 cup of salt

Mix the above ingredients. Then knead the dough well. When you can gather and roll it into a soft ball you are ready to create something special!

Paint and decorate your creation. Put your creation on display in your classroom gallery.

Media Link

Design a dream home with all the special features you would like to have in it.

Oops! You have to move!

Look in the real-estate section of a newspaper. Study the ads. Write your own advertisement for selling your home.

Design an "eye-catching" FOR SALE sign.

Wind
AND
Water

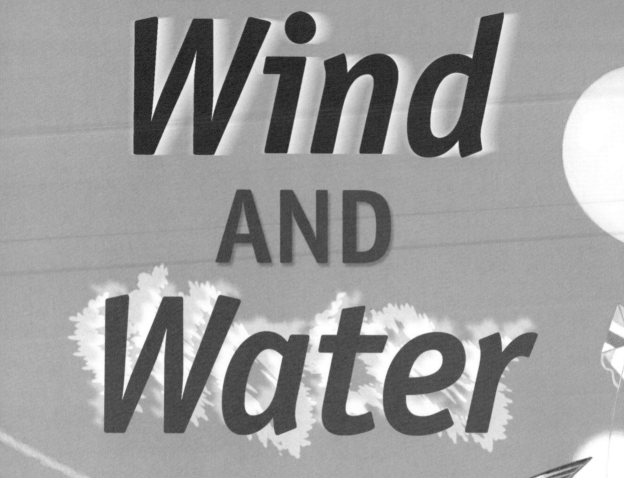

Balloon

By Colleen Thibaudeau

As
big as
ball as round
as sun ... I tug
and pull you when
you run and when
wind blows I
say polite
ly
H
O
L
D
M
E
T
I
G
H
T
L
Y.

Balloon Fiesta

by Tara Steele

Once a year, the skies over Sussex, New Brunswick, are filled with huge hot-air balloons. Over 30 000 people come to the Atlantic Balloon Festival to watch these amazing wonders.

Here you can watch as many as 30 colourful balloons rise in the air. Some balloons come in surprising shapes!

Hot-air balloons are made of nylon. They are very light and very strong.

efore the balloon goes up, the crew must get it ready.

First, the balloon is laid out on the ground and checked for holes. From end to end, it may be 18 metres long and nearly as wide!

Then the crew holds the mouth of the balloon open. The pilot starts the burner and aims the flame inside the balloon. As the air inside the balloon heats up, the balloon begins to rise. Soon it will be the size of a small house.

Balloons travel as fast or as slow as the wind. Balloon races test how well a pilot can move a balloon, not how fast it can go.

Pilots cannot steer their balloons. They can only make them go up or down. Wind moves in different directions and at different speeds at different levels. The pilot studies the wind and takes the balloon up or down to hit a stream of wind. Flying a balloon is a lot like sailing a boat.

Wherever the balloon travels, a truck or van follows it on the ground. That way, when the balloon lands, the pilot and the balloon have a ride home.

Balloons fly only in the early morning and early evening when the wind is light. During the day, the sun heats the air too much. Air that is too warm can cause a balloon to fall to the ground.

At night, the balloons are tied to the ground. With all their burners lit, the glowing balloons are an awesome sight.

A Balloon for Grandad

by Nigel Gray   pictures by Jane Ray

It was a warm day, so the back door stood wide
open. Sam's balloon snuggled up against the ceiling.
It was bobbing and bumping in the breeze.

After breakfast, Sam and Dad went upstairs to wash their hands. Then from the bathroom window Dad caught sight of a glint of silver and red.

"Look! There goes your balloon," he said. "It must have blown out the back door!"

They watched it rising up as straight and smooth as an elevator on its way to the very top floor of a building taller than the tallest tree.

They ran downstairs and went outside. Up and
up went the balloon, jerkily, fidgety now, in fits and
starts like a rock climber zigzagging up a cliff.

And then, when it was so high that it looked like
a tiny red berry in the sky, the wind grabbed it.

"I want my balloon," Sam cried.

"No!" said the wind. "It's mine! All mine!" And
off rushed the balloon, in a hurry now, south,
toward the mountains.

"Don't cry," said Dad. "Across the mountains is the sea, and across the sea is the desert, and across the desert, a river, and in the river, an island."

"And on that island," said Sam, "my grandad Abdulla lives, looking after his goats and tending his date trees."

"That's right," said Dad.

"Perhaps," said Sam, "my balloon is going to visit Grandad Abdulla."

"Yes," said Dad. "Then it will fly high, high, high over the snow-decorated mountains where golden eagles nest, high, high over the sparkling blue-green sea where silver fish leap from the waves...

...high over the hot yellow sand of the desert where scorpions and spitting spiders and sidewinder snakes hide from the heat."

"And sand grouse will peck at it," said Sam, "and falcons will fall on it, and hawks will fly after it, and vultures with their big hooky beaks and their sharp talons will tear at it, but the dry desert wind will help it to dodge and weave, and nothing will harm it."

"That's right," said Dad. "And then, tired after its long journey, it will see down below the long blue ribbon of the river; it will see the small gold-and-emerald jewel of the island; it will see the little brown house built of baked mud."

"Yes," said Sam, "and it will see Grandad Abdulla
sitting in the shade of his mango tree. And down,
down, down it will glide, landing in the yard like a
seagull settling on the sea.

And Grandad Abdulla will say, 'A balloon for me! My grandson Sam must have sent it to show that although he's so far away, he's thinking of me.'"

"Yes. It's sad to see it go," said Dad, "but the balloon will be happy after its great adventure. And Grandad Abdulla will be happy thinking of you."

"I'm glad my balloon's gone to see Grandad," said Sam, "because if I know Grandad's happy, then I feel happy too."

Twirling Toy

by Deborah Hodge

Make this toy helicopter and watch it fly. It's actually a simple machine that makes a soft landing every time.

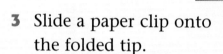

YOU WILL NEED

a piece of paper 18 x 5 cm
a pencil, scissors, and a paper clip

WHAT TO DO

1 Lay the paper strip over the pattern below. Trace the solid cutting and dotted folding lines.

2 Cut the solid lines A and B. Fold along the dotted lines C and D. Fold along the dotted line E.

3 Slide a paper clip onto the folded tip.

4 Cut the solid line F. Bend flap G back and flap H forward as shown.

5 Lift your toy helicopter up high and let it go. How does it move? Try flying it from a higher spot.

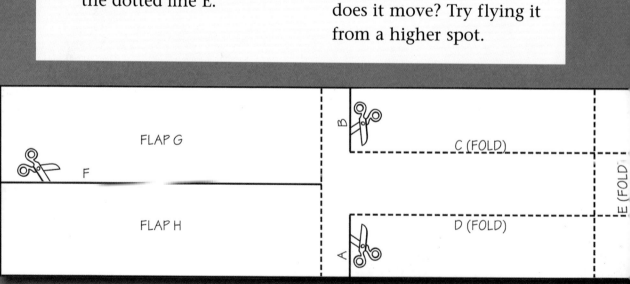

FLAP G

F

B

C (FOLD)

E (FOLD)

FLAP H

A

D (FOLD)

WHAT'S HAPPENING?
The toy helicopter twirls in a spiral as it drops. Turning in a spiral allows the helicopter to drop with less force. It lands softly instead of crashing down.

Rachel's Boat

by Niko Scharer

Clever little Rachel B.
Built herself a boat,
But when she sailed it out to sea
She found it wouldn't float.

The water rose above her toes
And right up to her chin.
And Rachel found a little hole
Was letting water in.

She didn't have a milking bowl,
A bucket or a pail.
She didn't have a single thing
That she could use to bail.

But Rachel was a clever soul.
She did not scream or shout,
But calmly cut another hole
To let the water out.

Follow the Water from Brook to Ocean

by
Arthur Dorros

After the next big rainstorm, put your boots on and go outside. Look at the water dripping from your roof. Watch it gush out of the drainpipes.

You can see water flowing down your street, too.

Water always flows downhill. It flows from high places to low places, just the way you and your skateboard move down a hill.

Where does the water start? Where does the water in a brook or a stream or a river come from?

The water comes from rain. And it comes from melting snow.

Some of it soaks into the ground, and some water is soaked up by trees and other plants. But a lot of the water keeps travelling over the ground, flowing downhill.

Trickles of water flow together to form a brook. A brook isn't very deep or wide. You could easily step across a brook to get to the other side.

Plop! A frog jumps into the brook.
Lots of creatures live in the moving water.

The brook flows into a stream. Water from many brooks feeds the stream.

A stream is big enough for a canoe. The water can move fast in a mountain stream! The stream bubbles and roars, racing downhill.

The fast-moving water is powerful. It carries along ground-up rock and soil. Big, heavy rocks get swept along too.

Sploosh! An otter slides down the steep bank of the stream.

The stream flows into a river. The river is deep and wide. Big boats can use the river. People can swim in it.

When a river comes to a rocky cliff, the water falls over the edge. It's a waterfall!

Sometimes a river overflows its banks, and it floods. Heavy rains might cause a river to flood. A flood can destroy people's homes and wash away a lot of soil.

Water may travel over land for thousands of
kilometres before it finally reaches the ocean. The
ocean holds most of the earth's water, and covers
almost three-quarters of the whole earth.

The ocean is so big, and so deep,
that it has hardly been explored.

The water has reached the end of its downhill trip. Water flowed from a brook, to a stream, to a river. It was a long journey to the ocean.

The next time you see water in a brook, a stream, or a river, you will know where it is going.

Wonderful Water

Why do we need to have water?

All living things need water to live. Without enough water, plants, animals, and people would die. Most of your body (60%) is made up of water. To stay healthy, you need to drink plenty of liquids to replace the water your body loses each day.

Why do we have waves?

When the wind blows across the top of the water, it creates ripples or little waves. In a light wind, the ripples may be quite small. In a strong wind, the water piles up to make larger waves that can be bigger than a house.

Why do I float in seawater?

Seawater has a lot of salt in it. The salt makes the water dense so that anything in it floats more easily. When you swim in seawater, you do not sink because the salt water supports your weight.

Sailboat

by Judy Press   pictures by Michael Kline

• •

Sailors navigate with stars to show them where they are.
If the winds are very calm, their boats don't go too far!

Here's what you need
2 large milk cartons
stapler
straw
construction paper scrap
tape
scissors
nail or pointed tool

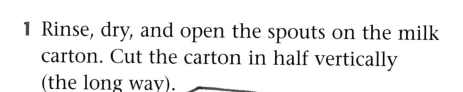

1 Rinse, dry, and open the spouts on the milk
   carton. Cut the carton in half vertically
   (the long way).

2 Reshape the remaining spout and staple it closed for a boat.

3 Cut the second carton in half horizontally and use the nail to poke a small hole in the bottom. Cut a slit in the straw.

4 Tape the half carton upside down in the boat. Push the uncut end of the straw into the hole for a mast. Cut a sail from paper and slide it into the slit on the straw. Use tape to hold it.

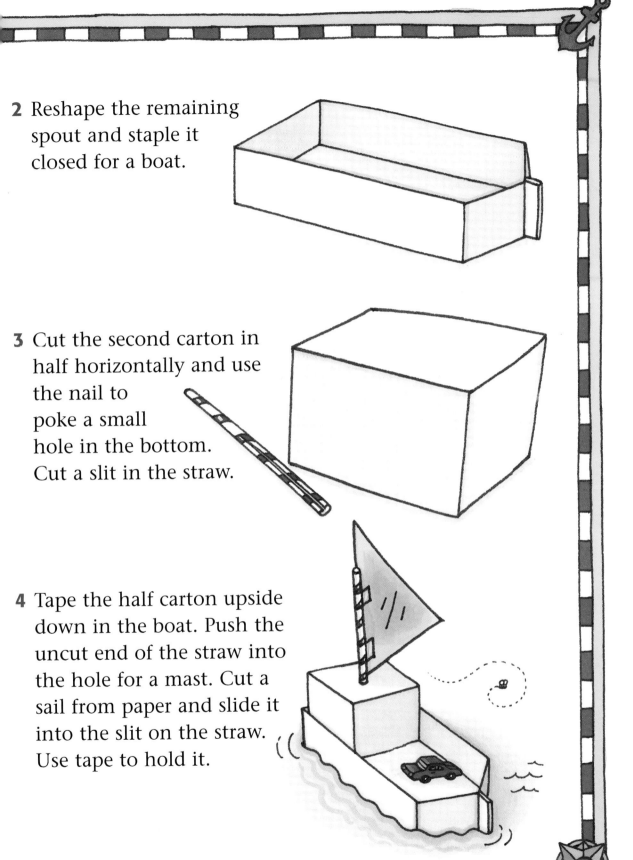

Media Link

You Found a Message in a Bottle!

At the seashore, you found a message in a bottle.

Write a story that answers these questions:

- When did you find it?
- Where did it come from?
- What does the message say?
- Who wrote it?
- Why did that person write it?
- What did you do?

Tape-record your story for others to listen to.

Who's in the Bottle?

- Write clues about yourself on a piece of paper.

- Roll it up and put it in an unbreakable, wide-mouthed bottle.

- Your teacher will give you a number to use instead of your name. Put your number on the outside of the bottle.

- Have fun with all your classmates by guessing who's in each bottle.

- Record your bottle guesses on a tally sheet.

- Keep your guesses "bottled up" until everyone has had a chance to play the guessing game.

Talk a Tale

You and your friend went on a hot-air balloon ride. You talked all through the trip. What did you say? Cut out 12 speech bubbles from a piece of blank paper.

On your speech bubbles write what you and your friend said during your cartoon balloon trip.

When your speech bubbles are complete, design your own cartoon adventure and paste in your speech bubbles.

Water Wash

On a piece of white paper, use crayons to draw sailboats on the water. Colour in the sails using every colour in the rainbow but blue. You must press very hard with your colours so that the colours are as bright as they can be. Mix blue water-colour paint with water to create a wash. With a paintbrush, spread your wash over the sailboat drawing.

Make sure that you cover the entire page. Display your picture on a bulletin board and give it a title.

My Country, My World

O Canada!

O Canada!
Our home and native land!

True patriot love,
in all thy sons command.

With glowing hearts,
we see thee rise,
The True North strong and free!

From far and wide,
O Canada,
we stand on guard for thee.

God keep our land,
glorious and free!

O Canada,
we stand on guard for thee.

O Canada,
we stand on guard for thee.

O Canada!
Terre de nos aïeux,

Ton front est ceint
de fleurons glorieux!

Car ton bras
sait porter l'épée,
Il sait porter
la croix!

Ton histoire
est une épopée
Des plus
brillants exploits.

Et ta valeur,
de foi trempée,

Protégera nos foyers
et nos droits,
Protégera nos foyers
et nos droits.

Crazy for Canada

by Noa Schwartz   pictures by Mick Beaumont and Susan Tebbutt

Lester B. Beaver reporting from all across the nation, with pictures of the places that I went on my vacation.

Did You Know...
that the first Canadian stamp, issued in 1851, had a picture of a beaver building a dam?

I started in the West
on the top of mountain peaks.
I thought that I'd try skiing
but my tail was sore for weeks.

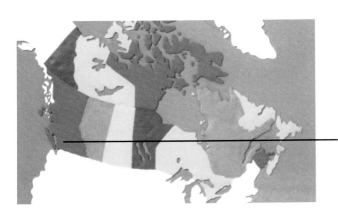

Whistler,
British Columbia

So to the Prairies I went next.
Can you see me hiding?
The flatlands full of wheat fields
were great for horseback riding.

Did You Know...
that the annual
Canadian wheat crop
could produce 6 billion
loaves of bread?

Winnipeg, Manitoba

Next I travelled to the North
to the land of the midnight sun,
to do some fishing on the ice.
It was great when I caught one.

Did You Know...
that Iqaluit, Nunavut,
gets 20 hours of sunlight
every June 21st?

Dawson, Yukon

Iqaluit, Nunavut
Yellowknife,
Northwest Territories

A snorting bull at the rodeo
was courteous indeed.
He found a special seat for me
at the world famous Stampede.

Did You Know...
that Calgary, Alberta, once
earned the nickname
"Cowtown" because it was
famous for the number of
cows roaming the streets?

Calgary, Alberta

Mounties in their uniforms—
Don't I look like one?

Regina,
Saskatchewan

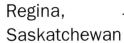

Cheering at a hockey game,
where we are number one!

Montréal, Québec

Off to the metropolis
to check out other sights—
to climb the tallest tower
and to reach the highest heights.

Did You Know...
that the CN Tower in
Toronto, Ontario, is the
tallest free-standing
structure in the world?

Toronto, Ontario

Canada, O Canada—
a thought from Lester B.
I will stand on guard forever
for "the True North strong
and free"!

———— Ottawa, Ontario

While fishing in the Maritimes
it became so clear to me,
from Pacific to Atlantic
there's no place I'd rather be.

Did You Know...
that Canada's official motto
is From Sea to Sea?

ATLANTIC CANADA
Charlottetown, Prince Edward Island
St. John's, Newfoundland
Saint John, New Brunswick
Halifax, Nova Scotia

Claudia's Coin

The Royal Canadian Mint makes all the money that Canadians use. The Mint had a contest asking Canadians to design new 25 cent coins to celebrate Canada's past and future. More than 60 000 people sent in their ideas for these new Millennium coins!

One coin was chosen for each month. June's coin shows the Canadian Pacific Railway, and the

coin for July shows different jobs that Canadians have. December's coin shows mountains, prairies, and water.

Claudia Bertrand, from Beauport, Québec, designed September's coin. Claudia was ten years old when she sent in her picture. She is the youngest person ever to design a Canadian coin.

Claudia's coin shows three people holding hands. This is what Claudia said when we asked her about it.

Claudia speaks French. We translated her answers into English for you to read.

Interviewer: Claudia, why did you enter the contest?

Claudia: I read about the contest on a flyer that came in the mail. I decided to enter because I like to draw.

Interviewer: How did you find out your design was chosen?

Claudia: I was at my friend's house and my mom called to tell me she had a surprise for me. When I got home, she told me my picture was chosen. I was really happy.

Interviewer: Tell us about your design.

Claudia: It is called "Canada Through a Child's Eye." The three people are living in harmony. I think peace and friendship are very important.

Interviewer: Were there any special events to celebrate your new coin?

Claudia: We had an assembly at my school. Everyone brought in a quarter and exchanged it for the new one I designed.

Canada's Maple Leaf
The Story of Our Flag

by **Ann-Maureen Owens**
and **Jane Yealland**

pictures by **Bill Slavin**
and **Esperança Melo**

In 1964, with Canada's 100th birthday only three years away, Prime Minister Lester B. Pearson decided it was time for Canada to have its own flag. He organized a flag committee.

Thousands of people sent in ideas. The flag committee room was soon filled with bags and bags of mail containing letters and drawings from across Canada, and even from Canadians living outside the country. As members of the committee chose their favourite designs, they stuck them on the walls of the committee room. Soon the room was covered with hundreds of designs.

What flag design would you have sent in?

By far, the majority of designs involved a maple leaf. Some showed 12 leaves to represent the provinces and territories, and many colours were used besides red. The beaver, Mounties on horseback, religious symbols, and the buffalo were some of the other suggestions.

Some symbols were unusual, including rabbits, eagles, Canada geese, and even hockey sticks.

First the committee divided its favourite designs into three groups.

Then the committee had to choose one of these groups.

Imagine how surprised they were when the votes were counted and they had all chosen the same category—the single maple leaf.

To Be a Kid

by **Maya Ajmera and
John D. Ivanko**

FAMILIES

Even though families
speak different
languages and express
things in different
ways, love and care
and kindness are
shared across cultures.

You may live with parents, grandparents, aunts, or cousins. But no matter what, families are there to help you grow and to protect you from trouble.

FUN

Around the world, everybody likes to have fun. You might enjoy climbing a tree or swinging on a jungle gym or just making funny faces.

"Goofing off" at the beach or balancing on the seesaw with your friends makes you smile and laugh until your stomach hurts.

FRIENDS

Friends talk and laugh and work and play wherever they live. They share discoveries and secrets and favourite snacks.

They help
each other by
understanding
and listening
to each other's
problems.
Friends are a
very important
part of life.

This Is the Way We Go to School

A Story About Children Around the World

by Edith Baer   pictures by Steve Björkman

One by one or two by two—
come along, it's fun to do!

Liz and Larry, as a rule,
wear their jogging shoes to school.

But the fastest way by far
is by school bus or by car!

Bianca, Beppo, Benedetto
ride aboard the vaporetto.

Bundled up against the breeze,
Niels and Solveig go on skis.

Palm trees help keep Ahmed cool
on his sunny walk to school.

Kay and Fay and Flo and Joe
go to school by radio.

William comes ashore by boat,
counting sea gulls while afloat.

And the famous Metro line
suits Igor and Ilyana fine.

Go by 'copter?

by Ski-Doo?

Somewhere, sometimes, some kids do!

You come too!
We'll look for you.

Mabel Murple

by Sheree Fitch
pictures by Maryann Kovalski

What if ...

There was a purple planet

With purple people on it

Would those purple people play

Whatever purple way they wanted

And what if...

EVERYTHING was purple
I mean a WHOLE PURPLE WORLD
And there was someone just like me
I mean a purple sort of girl

And if...

There was a purple girl
How purple could she be?
Would she get in purple trouble?
(She would, if she were me!)

Now...
This purple girl should have a name
What name could rhyme with purple?
I must dream up a proper name...
I'VE GOT IT!

Now that I have named her
I will dream of what she's like...
Would Mabel Murple ride upon
Her purple motorbike?

Mabel Murple's house was purple
So was Mabel's hair
Mabel Murple's dog was purple
A purple poodle named Pierre

Mabel Murple had a skateboard
She skittered down the street
She wore a pair of purple sneakers
Upon her purple feet

Mabel Murple ordered breakfast
She had purple eggs on toast
And when she ordered dinner
She had purple short-rib roast

Mabel Murple's room was purple
So was Mabel's bed
She slept with purple pillows
Beneath her purple head

She wore purple-dot pyjamas
And polka-purple socks
She had a purple teddy bear
Named Snickerknickerbox!

(And he SNORED!)

Even Mabel Murple
Has to close her eyes
I wonder if she dreams
Of distant purple skies?

Perhaps she dreams of places
She has never been
Of a world with multicolours
That she has never seen

Or perhaps when Mabel Murple
dreams
She dreams of...

Gertrude Green!

Gertrude Green!
Gertrude Green's house was green
So was Gertrude's hair
Gertrude Green's cat was green
So was her...

Lester B. Beaver's Photo Album

Using old magazines and travel brochures, find and cut out pictures of places Lester B. Beaver visited.

1. Make a photo album of his journey.

2. Draw Lester on the first page. Give the album a title.

3. Label each page by territory or province.

4. Include 3 or 4 photos of places in each area.

WORD SEARCH

Check in "Crazy for Canada" if you need help finding the hidden names of places in Canada.

Print your answers on an interesting Canadian shape, such as a maple leaf or beaver.

b	l	H	q	c	Q	i	M	a	r	i	t	i	m	e	s	e	a	o	k
k	d	a	s	w	d	u	k	p	k	s	w	n	u	b	e	u	l	z	T
p	o	l	n	i	t	g	é	j	h	W	i	n	n	i	p	e	g	r	o
e	n	i	a	b	l	j	e	b	a	x	l	r	e	p	y	m	g	k	r
P	u	f	w	o	y	q	t	g	e	o	v	a	w	n	r	l	u	c	o
r	h	a	c	f	r	p	a	r	h	c	j	D	a	w	s	o	n	q	n
a	z	x	j	m	h	n	o	z	a	w	d	l	k	f	r	b	d	o	t
i	p	l	s	z	i	f	a	r	d	z	j	i	n	h	m	r	e	m	o
r	y	u	x	g	k	z	y	u	y	b	f	k	A	k	x	e	i	w	c
i	d	v	e	p	b	r	y	s	j	v	a	e	m	l	q	i	y	p	o
e	o	R	t	r	a	g	p	f	i	q	m	r	g	a	b	n	p	b	a
s	n	p	q	g	l	W	h	i	s	t	l	e	r	k	l	e	d	t	r
q	b	u	l	t	p	p	d	e	w	g	l	z	q	p	c	a	r	g	u
g	m	a	o	f	N	e	w	f	o	u	n	d	l	a	n	d	i	t	v
f	C	l	c	s	x	o	d	v	y	g	l	w	p	d	h	j	k	g	a

Kid Stories

Here are some story ideas. Choose one or use an idea of your own. Write a story.

- The Planet Where Only Kids Live
- I Travelled Back in Time and Met My Great-great-grandma
- How to Be a Great Kid

When I Was a Kid

Interview your teacher or family members. Ask them about their best memories of being a kid. Tape-record or write about your interview in an interesting way.

Let's Go Somewhere in the World

You and a classmate are going to visit your pen pal in another country.

- Make a little suitcase from a box. Put a travel label on it.
- Make a plane ticket.
- Pack your suitcase with cutout clothes and other things to show what you will need to take with you.

Find out all you can about the country you will visit.

- Look on the globe.
- Do research about the country in the library.
- Find out about the climate.
- Find out about the food.
- Find out about the land.
- Find out about the language. (Look in the 300 section of the library.)

Celebrate Reading

On a Day in Summer

by Aileen Fisher

On a day in summer
where the path made a crook,
a boy leaned on a boulder
and opened a book.

He didn't hear the cricket
on the meadow's floor,
he didn't hear the fledglings
begging, "More, more, more."

He didn't feel the shadow
sliding down the tree,
he didn't see the closeness
of a bumblebee.

He didn't see the rabbit
or smell the yellow clover...
he wasn't even hungry
till the book was over.

Reading
All Around Us

CORN NUGGETS

The Golden Nuggets You Can Eat!

9 Vitamins and Minerals No Sugar Added

Great New Taste!

EXIT

STOP

Hiking Bound

The Right Shoe

Great Paths Ahead

Meet the

Painted Words

by Aliki Brandenberg

Marianthe knew this day would come.
  Now that it was here, she didn't know if she
would laugh or cry.

"I won't know anyone," she said again.

"Most people don't know anyone at a new school," said Mama.

"I won't understand what they say," said Marianthe. "You will look and listen and learn," said Mama.

"They won't understand me," said Marianthe.

"A body can talk," said Mama. "Eyes speak many words, and a smile is a smile in any language." "Everything here is so different," said Marianthe. "Only on the outside," said Mama. "Inside, people are the same."

"I am a little afraid," said Marianthe. "But not enough to cry."

Marianthe felt hot and frozen at the same time.
She did not understand when the tall teacher said,
"We are delighted to have you, Marianthe. May we
call you Mari?"

But she understood when he bent down and
shook her hand.

She did not understand when he said, "This is our new teammate, Mari," or when the children said, "Good morning, Mari." But she understood when he led her to her own desk and when some of the children smiled, and others waved.

Today is Monday, September 3.
We have a new girl in class.
Her name is Marianthe, or Mari.
She comes from

The tall teacher wrote words on the board.
They looked like sticks and chicken feet,
humps and moons.
Mari could just look.
He read from a book.
Words changed with his voice.

They sounded like sputters
and coughs and whispering
wind.
The words made the children
laugh, and say "ahhh" or "ooh."
Mari could just listen.

Suddenly everyone jumped up and scattered around the room.

Some piled blocks into towers.

Others lumped clay into shapes or threaded pasta.

"Misapeechi," Mari heard.

"Misapeechi. Misapeechi," she heard again and again.

Each time the teacher answered, and Mari understood. This was his name.

Misapeechi swept the air with his arm, and again Mari understood.

She went straight to an easel and began to paint.

"Mari is an artist," said Rachel.

"High marks for observation," said Misapeechi.

The next day Mari looked and listened.
During Creating Time, she painted again.

"Mari is telling us something," said Albert.

"She is talking with her paints," said Rachel.

"There's more than one way to peel an orange,"
said Misapeechi. "And there is more than one way
to tell a story. Someday Mari will be able to tell us
with words."

Every day when Mari went home, Mama listened and learned.

She heard about the many different things that were becoming familiar to Mari—voice sounds and counting numbers and writing those funny sticks that were also in the schoolbooks they read.

"And every day I draw another picture," Mari told Mama. "It's my story about us. I am drawing what I can't talk."

Mari told Mama of tall Misapeechi, and of Waisha and Kista and Ahbe, who smiled and spoke with their eyes and talked with their hands so she could understand.

And she told of the other ones. "In life there will always be those who hurt and tease out of ignorance," said Mama. "You look and listen so you will not be one of them."

Patik was the worst.

That day she was hurt enough to cry, but she didn't. She painted instead.

That day everyone understood Mari's painting, even Patik.

"We have here a great deal to talk about," said Misapeechi. "Let our ideas begin."

Slowly, like clouds lifting, things became clearer.
Sticks and chicken feet became letters.
Sputters and coughs became words.
And the words had meanings.
Every day Mari understood
more and more.
Misapeechi became Mr. Petrie.
Waisha became Rachel, Kista
became Kristin, Ahbe became
Albert, and Patik became Patrick.

One day Mr. Petrie clipped a heap of paintings to the wall.

"The time has come for patience to be rewarded," he said. "Ready, Mari?"

"Ready," said Mari.

She told her story in her new words, page by painted page, as she would read a book.

When she finished, the class clapped and
cheered.

"Bravo! More!" they shouted. "We want more!"

"We shall have more," said Mr. Petrie. "I have
a strong suspicion that we have here a class of
writers, each with a story to tell."

"I have one," said Kristin.

"I have one," said Patrick.

"And we'll call our classroom Writers Galore."

Mari was so excited, her heart skipped beats as she told Mama.

"And look at you, Mama," she said.

Mama was writing in her book, copying letters into words into meanings.

"You have looked and listened and learned well, Mama," said Mari.

"Soon you will be writing your own story. Just think what Mr. Petrie will say!"

PEN PALS

Pen pals are friends who write letters to each other from different places in the world.

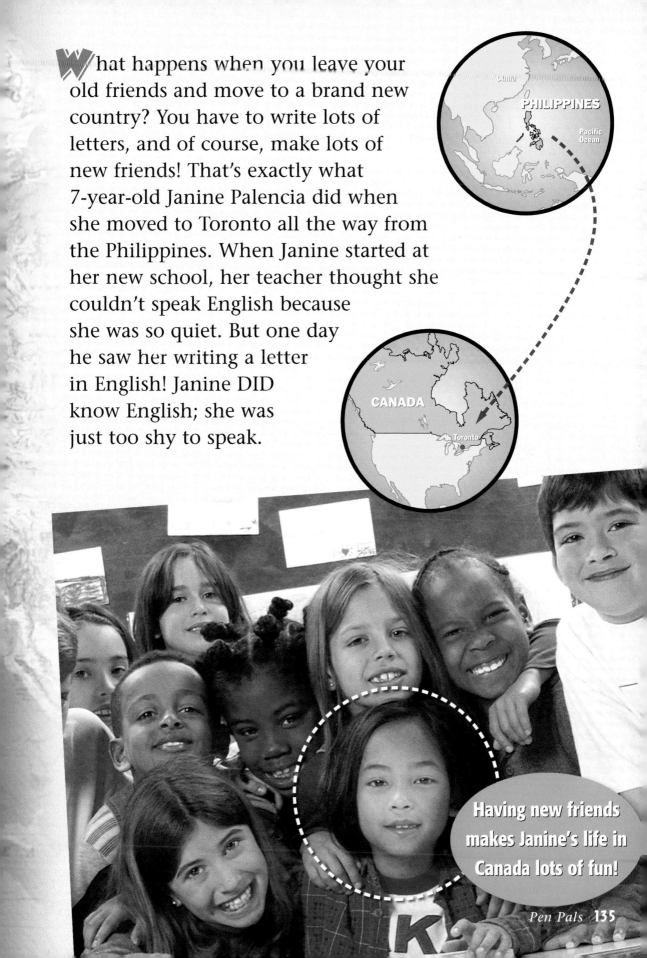

What happens when you leave your old friends and move to a brand new country? You have to write lots of letters, and of course, make lots of new friends! That's exactly what 7-year-old Janine Palencia did when she moved to Toronto all the way from the Philippines. When Janine started at her new school, her teacher thought she couldn't speak English because she was so quiet. But one day he saw her writing a letter in English! Janine DID know English; she was just too shy to speak.

Having new friends makes Janine's life in Canada lots of fun!

Dear Mr. Blueberry

by Simon James

Dear Mr. Blueberry,

I love whales very much and I think I saw one in my pond today. Please send me some information on whales, as I think he might be hurt.

Love,
Emily

Dear Emily,

Here are some details about whales. I don't think you'll find it was a whale you saw, because whales don't live in ponds, but in salt water.

Yours sincerely,
Your teacher,
Mr. Blueberry

Dear Mr. Blueberry,

I am now putting salt into the pond every day before breakfast, and last night I saw my whale smile. I think he is feeling better. Do you think he might be lost?

Love,
Emily

Dear Emily,

Please don't put any more salt in the pond. I'm sure your parents won't be pleased. I'm afraid there can't be a whale in your pond, because whales don't get lost. They always know where they are in the oceans.

Yours sincerely,
Mr. Blueberry

Dear Mr. Blueberry,

Tonight I am very happy because I saw my whale jump up and spurt lots of water. He looked blue. Does this mean he might be a blue whale?

Love,
Emily

P.S. What can I feed him?

Dear Emily,

Blue whales are blue and they eat tiny shrimplike creatures that live in the sea. However, I must tell you that a blue whale is much too big to live in your pond.

Yours sincerely,
Mr. Blueberry

P.S. Perhaps it is a blue goldfish?

Dear Mr. Blueberry,

Last night I read your letter to my whale. Afterward he let me stroke his head. It was very exciting. I secretly took him some crunched-up cornflakes and bread crumbs. This morning I looked in the pond and they were all gone. I think I shall call him Arthur. What do you think?

Love,
Emily

Dear Emily,

I must point out to you quite forcibly now that in no way could a whale live in your pond. You may not know that whales are migratory, which means they travel great distances each day. I am sorry to disappoint you.

Yours sincerely,

Mr. Blueberry

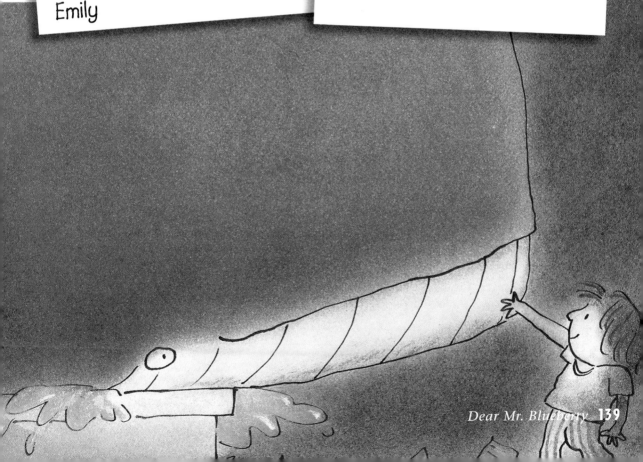

Dear Mr. Blueberry,
    Tonight I'm a little sad. Arthur has gone. I think your letter made sense to him and he has decided to be migratory again.
Love,
Emily

Dear Emily,
    Please don't be too sad, it really was impossible for a whale to live in your pond. Perhaps when you are older you would like to sail the oceans studying and protecting whales.
    Yours sincerely,
    Mr. Blueberry

Dear Mr. Blueberry,

It's been the happiest day! I went to the beach and you'll never guess, but I saw Arthur! I called to him and he smiled. I knew it was Arthur because he let me stroke his head. I gave him some of my sandwich and then we said good-bye. I shouted that I loved him very much and, I hope you don't mind, I said you loved him, too.

Love,
Emily (and Arthur)

"Come Quick!"

by Sue Alexander

THE PLAY BEGINS

The father is sitting in a chair in his living room.
He is reading a book. The boy comes running in.

BOY   Father! Come quick! There's a gorilla in
my room!

The father looks up from his book.

FATHER   Don't be silly. That's a joke. Of course there is no gorilla in your room!

He reads his book again.

BOY   But, Father, the gorilla is jumping up and down—like this!

The boy jumps up and down and scratches himself as a gorilla would.

FATHER   I must say, you make a very good gorilla! But now I want to read my book. Go to your room and find something to do.

The boy goes out slowly. He runs back in.

BOY   Father! Now there's a snake in my room, too! He is wriggling around and saying HSSSSSS!

The father puts down his book and stands up.

FATHER   That's enough! First you tell me that there is a gorilla in your room! That he is jumping around like this!

He jumps around like a gorilla.

Now you tell me there is a snake in your room! And he is saying HSSSS! Those are just silly stories! And I want to read my book. Go to your room!

The boy goes out slowly. The father sits down and reads his book again. The boy runs back in.

BOY   Father! PLEASE come quick! Now there is a seal in my room! And he is saying GWARK! And he is clapping his fins together—like this!

The boy bounces like a seal and claps his hands.

GWARK! GWARK!

FATHER   Hmmm. Maybe I had better go and look after all. If those animals ARE in your room, we will have to call the zoo!

He puts down his book and gets up and goes out.

BOY   Ha! Ha! I did it! I made him look! And there's nothing there! What a good joke!

The father runs back in, very excited.

FATHER   You were right! There IS a seal in your room! And a snake! And a gorilla! AND THEY ARE ALL ON YOUR BED! We had better call the zoo!

The boy jumps up. He is surprised at what his father has said.

BOY   WHAT! How can that be! I'd better go see!

He runs out. He comes back carrying pictures of a seal, a snake, and a gorilla. He is smiling.

FATHER   Gotcha!

They laugh and go off together.

Bedbunnies

by Bonnie Christensen

Though I'm the bravest kid in town,

I don't a+ [door] those nighttime sounds.

They make my courage start to [sink] .

I [shutter] and forget to blink.

Beneath my bed I slowly [peer] .

What do you s'pose is rumbling there?

Dustbunnies big, dustbunnies small,

rowdy dustbunnies  to  .

Should I  them with my mop?

Or join them in the bunny hop?

door   sink   shutter   stair   wall   nail

Firefly Song

An Ojibwa poem

Flitting white-fire insects!
Wandering small-fire beasts!
Wave little stars about my bed!
Weave little stars into my sleep!

Come, little dancing white-fire bug!
Come, little flitting white-fire beast!
Light me with your white-flame magic,
Your little star-torch.

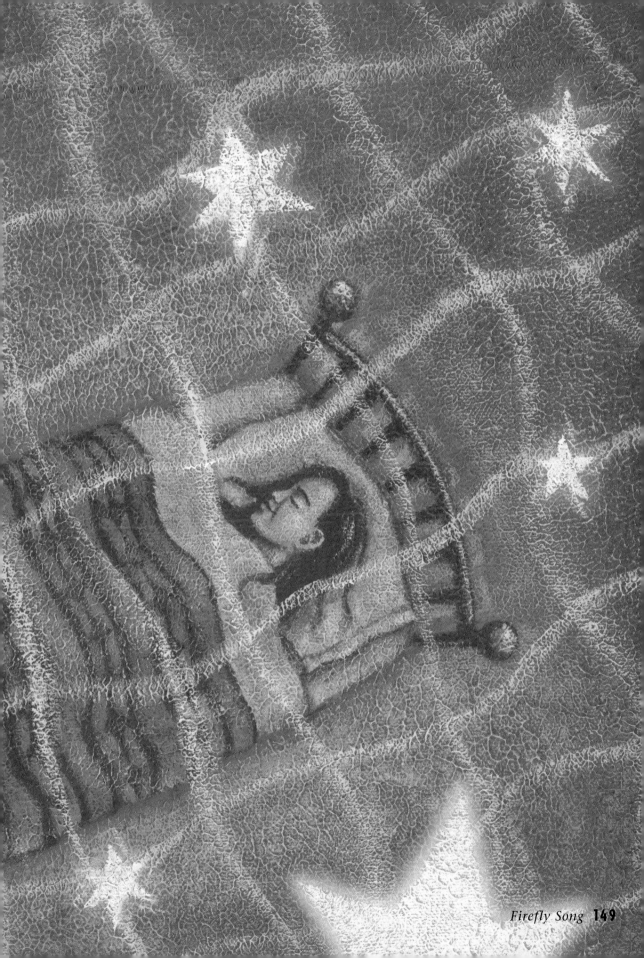

Reading Grows

by **Ellen B. Senisi**

Reading grows—bit by bit...

...picture by picture.

Reading grows—colour by colour...

Blue, yellow, red, orange, purple, green—what's your favourite colour?

...story by story.

"When we're done, please read it again. And don't skip any words this time."

"This is my favourite part!"

Reading grows—letter by letter...

"I know every letter in my name!"

...word by word...

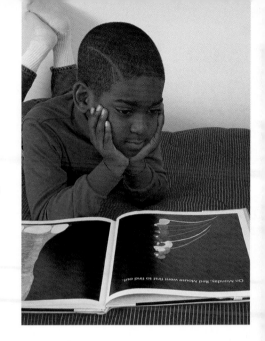

...sentence by sentence.

"Now let's read together."

Reading grows— book by book...

...by book, by book,
and before you know it,
you enter the world of books.

**You learn
what you always
wanted to know.**

You read stories, you write your own stories, and you can help someone else learn to read.

Reading grows—just like you!

HEY GANG!

Whales travel in groups called pods.

Which of these animals would you see in

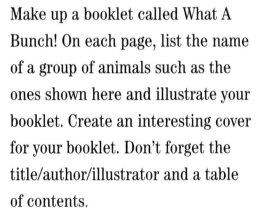

- a pride?
- a school?
- a flock?
- a gaggle?
- a herd?

Make up a booklet called What A Bunch! On each page, list the name of a group of animals such as the ones shown here and illustrate your booklet. Create an interesting cover for your booklet. Don't forget the title/author/illustrator and a table of contents.

Grow, Bookworm, Grow!

WHAT YOU NEED TO DO:

- Make a round, cardboard head for your bookworm.
- Make eyes, antennae, and a smile for your bookworm's head.
- Poke a small hole in the middle of your bookworm's face.
- Through this hole put the end of a piece of thick yarn (about 30 cm long).
- Knot the end of the yarn.... Now your bookworm has a nose!
- Cut out coloured paper circles the same size as your bookworm's head.

- On each circle, print the title of a book you have read.
- String this circle on your yarn.
- Add a new circle for every book you read.
- See how your bookworm grows!

SEE HOW YOUR READING GROWS!

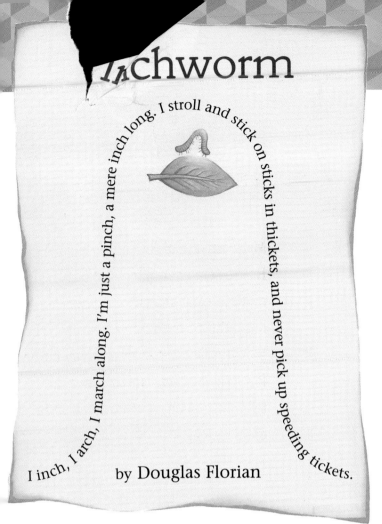

Inchworm

I inch, I arch, I march along. I'm just a pinch, a mere inch long. I stroll and stick on sticks in thickets, and never pick up speeding tickets.

by Douglas Florian

It's All In The Shape!

Shape poems are fun to look at and to read. Why did the poet create this shape? How do the words suit the shape?

Create your own shape poem. Share it with a friend.

Read All About It!

Extra, extra,
Read all about it.
We love our books.
And we're going to shout it!

What is your "best-ever" book?

- Fold a large piece of construction paper in half so that it looks like a book cover. Decorate the front of the cover so that it represents the best book you have read.

- Make up a commercial to advertise this book to your friends. Tell about all its features.

- Design a poster highlighting your book.

- Survey your classmates to discover their favourite books.

- Make a bulletin board to show your Top 20 Books. When all the posters are up, you and your friends will have lots of ideas for good books to read.